FAITH AND HEALTH DEVOTIONAL SERIES

REBUILD YOUR TEMPLE
GOD'S WAY®

BOOK 3: REALIGN YOUR SPIRIT

A 10-DAY JOURNEY TO
SPIRITUAL HEALTH AND WHOLENESS

STEPHANIE L. FRANKLIN-SUBER

Dedication

To my treasured husband, **Berchard V. Suber**, and my son, **Michael Franklin Suber**—bless you for your enduring love, prayers, and faith throughout every season of my health and faith journey.

You have stood beside me with steadfast courage and reminded me daily of God's unfailing mercy and grace.

To **Reverend Anna Grant-Borden** and to the members of **Mount Airy Presbyterian Church**, past, present, and future.

To every woman who has walked through a season of spiritual dryness or a crushed spirit—may you rediscover the nearness and serenity of the Holy Spirit, who breathes new life into weary hearts, rekindles faith, and restores hope where it has faded.

With unwavering gratitude to the **Holy Spirit** who aligns us with the Heavenly Father who loves and restores us and with His Son who redeems and renews us, so that we may live in His peace and His purpose.

May You be glorified.

Blessed by the support of Cathy Morenzie, Preston Squire, and Jennifer Eastmond, and by the gifted work of Alec Gerhart and Rachel Aponte.

Foreword

Do you not know that your body is a temple of the Holy Spirit who is within you, whom you have from God, and that you are not your own? You were bought with a price [you were actually purchased with the precious blood of Jesus and made His own]. So then, honor and glorify God with your body.
(1 Corinthians 6:19–20 AMP)

Our bodies are sacred edifices, masterfully created by God for His glory and for worship. In Psalm 19:1, King David declares, *"The heavens declare the glory of God; the skies proclaim the work of his hands."* Just as the heavens reflect the majesty of God, so do we — His beloved creation. We are the workmanship of His hands, *"fearfully and wonderfully made."*

Yet as we journey through life, the demands placed on our bodies — some self-imposed and others thrust upon us by circumstances, people, or illness — can leave us depleted, wounded, or disconnected from the God who created us. In these moments of weariness and brokenness, we stand in need of **restoration**, **renewal**, and **realignment** with our Creator.

In this beautifully architected and God-inspired devotional collection, Stephanie Franklin-Suber gently but powerfully guides you through a sacred journey to restore your body, renew your soul, and realign your spirit.

Stephanie has walked this very path — from brokenness into wholeness through the transformative power of God's Word. God miraculously healed and delivered her from cancer, from years of chronic illness, and most recently from cardiac arrest. In each chapter of her testimony, God revealed to her the sacredness of her temple and showed her that, through faith in Jesus Christ, through Scripture, and by the work of the Holy Spirit, her temple could be rebuilt — God's way. Today, God has called Stephanie to help others rebuild their temples: body, soul, and spirit.

It is with joy and deep gratitude that I introduce you to this ***Rebuild Your Temple, God's Way® Signature Faith and Health Collection***, which includes the three-book *10-Day Devotional Series* (*Restore Your Body*, *Renew Your Soul*, and *Realign Your Spirit*) and the two-book *30-Day Devotional Series* (the *30-Day Devotional* and the companion *Bible Study Workbook*).

As you embark on this sacred journey, do so with **anticipation** and **expectation**. Allow the Word of God to minister to your soul through Scripture and Reflection. Worship God with your body through the daily Temple

Practice. Receive God's healing and restoration by engaging the Health Coaching Tips. And experience spiritual alignment as your spirit connects with the Spirit of God through prayer and journaling in the *Rebuild Your Temple, God's Way® Journal.*

It is my honor and delight to invite you to experience this transformational journey.

Come, and Rebuild Your Temple, God's Way®.

Yours in Christ,
Rev. Anna L. Grant-Borden
Senior Pastor, Mt. Airy Presbyterian Church
Philadelphia, Pennsylvania

Table of Contents

Daily Devotionals
Each day includes Scripture, Reflection, Temple Practice, Health Coaching Tip, Prayer, Journal Prompt, and Affirmation.

You are encouraged to use the Rebuild Your Temple, God's Way® Journal or your own personal journal to capture your prayers, insights, and reflections each day.

Author's Introduction

There are moments in your health and faith journey when your spirit feels empty—when prayers seem to echo in silence, and your once-bright light of faith flickers in the darkness of loss, weariness, disappointment or uncertainty.

If you have ever felt spiritually disconnected or dry, you are not alone. The pages that follow were born from my own journey of rebuilding my temple, God's way. Through cancer, chronic illness, and even cardiac arrest, my spirit was crushed again and again—but each time, the Holy Spirit comforted me in my brokenness and realigned me. What He did for me; He can do for you. This devotional is your invitation to return—to reconnect with the Holy Spirit.

In the *Holiest of Holies*, the innermost part of the Temple of Jerusalem, God's presence once rested in the Ark of the Covenant behind a veil. Only the priest could enter to commune with the Most High God. But through the atoning sacrifice of His Son, Jesus Christ, that veil was torn, and His Holy Spirit now dwells within your Triune Human Temple™ (Body–Soul–Spirit). The Holy Spirit is not a distant mystery but your intimate companion—your Comforter, Counselor, and Guide through every season of your journey.

Book 1 – Restore Your Body focused on God the Father, your Creator and Provider.

*Book 2 – Renew Your Soul r*eflected the compassion of God the Son, your Shepherd and Healer.

This book – *Realign Your Spirit* – continues your Triune Temple Journey™ and brings you into communion with God the Holy Spirit, who connects you to the love and power of the Heavenly Father and aligns your heart and mind with the heart and mind of Christ so that you can walk in the fullness of your divine purpose.

During this 10-day journey, you will rediscover what it means to dwell in the presence of the Holy Spirit, listen for His voice, and live guided by His peace. You will move from spiritual dryness to divine alignment—from feeling distant from God to living daily in the Fruit of the Holy Spirit.

Each day includes:

- **Scripture** to anchor your spiritual awareness,
- **Reflection** to deepen your spiritual sensitivity,
- **Temple Practice** to experience the Holy Spirit,
- **Health Coaching Tip** for spiritual balance and holistic health,
- **Prayer** to invite the comfort, guidance and empowerment of the Holy Spirit,
- **Journal Prompt** to nurture hearing the voice of the Spirit and self-reflection, and
- **Affirmation** to declare alignment with God's will.

May you encounter the gentle whisper of the Holy Spirit to breathe life into all your dry places. May your spirit be realigned, refreshed, and filled again with joy.

God the Holy Spirit invites you to go even deeper in this journey and realign your spirit—His way.

 DAY 1 – DWELL IN HIS PRESENCE

Scripture
The Lord is close to the brokenhearted and saves those who are crushed in spirit.
(Psalm 34:18 NIV)

Reflection
When the spirit is weary, even prayer can feel heavy. Silence may echo louder than the voice of God's Holy Spirit, and worship may feel distant. Yet this is where healing begins—in the quiet, not the noise.

Jesus Christ does not stand apart from your brokenness; He draws near to it. He does not scold you for feeling dry; He sits beside you in it. He gave you His Holy Spirit to comfort you.

Spiritual dryness is not the absence of faith—it is an invitation to return to dependence on the Holy Spirit. Nearness to the Spirit is not earned through effort; it is received through openness. When you simply sit before Him— no words, no performance—you begin to sense His steady presence again.

The Spirit breathes where there has been no breath, rekindling the flame that suffering tried to extinguish. The same Spirit who breathed life into creation now breathes peace into your soul.

Temple Practice
Find a quiet place. Sit still for five minutes and whisper, "Holy Spirit, I know You are near." Breathe slowly as you rest in that truth.

Health Coaching Tip
Stillness restores spiritual rhythm and lowers stress. Schedule a daily "pause moment" to breathe, release tension, and welcome the Holy Spirit's peace.

Prayer
Holy Spirit,
Draw near to my crushed spirit. Help me rest in Your presence until my heart feels Your peace again.
In Jesus' name, I pray, Amen.

Journal Prompt
When have you felt most aware of the Holy Spirit's presence in difficult times?

Affirmation
I am sustained by the Holy Spirit in me, even in my brokenness. He is as close as the breath I breathe.

 DAY 2 – ABIDE IN THE VINE

Scripture
Remain in me, as I also remain in you. No branch can bear fruit by itself; it must remain in the vine.
(John 15:4–5 NIV)

Reflection
Spiritual dryness often comes when we try to live disconnected from the Source. Like a branch separated from the vine, our strength fades when we rely on self-effort.

Abiding is not striving—it is surrendering. It means resting in the truth that God's Spirit flows continually, even when you cannot feel it. Your role is to stay connected. Every act of prayer, worship, or quiet trust allows His life to flow again.

Over time, you will notice renewal—not forced growth, but gentle fruit born from communion. In abiding, your crushed spirit becomes a living branch again, nourished by divine love.

Temple Practice
Visualize your heart as a branch connected to Christ the Vine. With each breath, imagine His life-giving Spirit flowing into you.

Health Coaching Tip
Stay hydrated. Water mirrors the Spirit's renewing flow. As you drink, thank the Holy Spirit for sustaining your body, soul, and spirit.

Prayer
Holy Spirit,
Help me remain in You when I feel weak or dry. Let Your life flow through me and make me fruitful again.
In Jesus' name, I pray, Amen.

Journal Prompt
Where in your spiritual life have you been striving instead of abiding?

Affirmation
I remain connected to Christ, and His Spirit renews my strength.

 DAY 3 – WALK BY THE SPIRIT

Scripture
Since we live by the Spirit, let us keep in step with the Spirit.
(Galatians 5:25 NIV)

Reflection
Realignment begins when you stop forcing your own rhythm and start walking in the Spirit's. After trauma or hardship, it is easy to become spiritually out of sync—rushing ahead or lagging behind in fear or fatigue. The Spirit invites you to walk, not run; to move, not drift.

When you walk by the Spirit, you let His timing become yours. Each step is guided by grace, not guilt. Some days, your pace will be slow—but even slow steps toward intimacy with the Spirit are sacred. The goal is not perfection; it is presence.

As you walk in step with the Spirit, you will find He restores balance where chaos once ruled and purpose where confusion lingered.

Temple Practice
Take a mindful walk. Match your breathing to your steps. With each exhale, whisper, "Holy Spirit, guide me."

Health Coaching Tip
Walking outdoors enhances mood and spiritual focus. Ten minutes of movement can clear mental fog and open your heart to prayer.

Prayer
Holy Spirit,
Align my pace with Yours. Teach me to walk in harmony with Your guidance every day.
In Jesus' name, I pray, Amen.

Journal Prompt
What does "keeping in step with the Spirit" look like in this season of your life?

Affirmation
I walk in rhythm with the Spirit, guided by His peace and purpose.

 DAY 4 – ALIGN WITH HIS WORD

Scripture
Your word is a lamp for my feet, a light on my path.
(Psalm 119:105 NIV)

Reflection
In seasons of spiritual dryness, feelings cannot always be trusted, but the Word always can. Scripture steadies you when emotions waver and lights your path when darkness lingers.

The Word realigns your spirit because it reveals God's triune character. Reading the Bible is not just a study—it is an encounter. Each verse is a window through which His Spirit shines. When your mind is weary and your hope is dim, open His Word as you would open a window to fresh air.

Let truth illuminate your confusion until peace returns to your spirit.

Temple Practice
Read Psalm 119:105 aloud. Then, write it in your journal, adding a short prayer: "Holy Spirit, align my steps with the Word today."

Health Coaching Tip
Morning Scripture reading before checking messages reduces stress and sets a positive mindset for the day.

Prayer
Holy Spirit,
Guide me and let Your Word light my path and anchor my thoughts in truth.
In Jesus' name, I pray, Amen.

Journal Prompt
How has Scripture recently corrected or comforted your spirit?

Affirmation
I am filled with the Holy Spirit who shines in me, lights my path, and aligns my spirit with His truth.

 DAY 5 – LISTEN FOR HIS VOICE

Scripture
My sheep listen to my voice; I know them, and they follow me.
(John 10:27 NIV)

Reflection
When life feels noisy, discerning the voice of the Holy Spirit can seem impossible. But His voice is not lost—it is simply waiting for space. The Holy Spirit often whispers, not because He is distant, but because He desires closeness.

To hear Him again, quiet the inner clutter of worry and distraction. The more you rest, the clearer His presence becomes. His voice is peace, not pressure; assurance, not accusation.

When your spirit learns to listen, you will realize He never stopped speaking—you just stopped hearing. Reconnection begins not with louder prayers, but with quieter hearts.

Temple Practice
Find a peaceful spot. Take three slow breaths. Whisper, "Speak, Holy Spirit. Your servant is listening." Wait in silence for one minute.

Health Coaching Tip
Noise fatigue increases stress hormones. Take short "sound fasts" throughout your day to rest your senses and attune your spirit.

Prayer
Holy Spirit,
Tune my ears to Your voice and quiet the noise within me. I long to hear and follow You closely.
In Jesus' name, I pray, Amen.

Journal Prompt
When was the last time you sensed the Holy Spirit speaking to your spirit?

Affirmation
I quiet and open my spirit. I hear the Holy Spirit's voice with peace and clarity.

DAY 6 – WORSHIP IN SPIRIT AND TRUTH

Scripture
Yet a time is coming and has now come when the true worshipers will worship the Father in the Spirit and in truth, for they are the kind of worshipers the Father seeks. (John 4:23–24 NIV)

Reflection
Worship is not a performance; it is participation in the life of the Spirit. When Jesus spoke these words to the Samaritan woman, He revealed that worship no longer depends on a temple built by hands—the Holy Spirit has made your spirit His dwelling place.

True worship happens when spirit meets Spirit: honesty replaces striving, surrender replaces routine. In pain or in praise, worship reconnects you to the God who never left. As you open your spirit to Him, the Spirit shifts your perspective, restoring joy where sorrow lingered.

Temple Practice
Play a worship song that draws you near to the Holy Spirit. As you sing or listen, focus on His presence rather than your performance.

Health Coaching Tip
Singing slows the breath and lowers stress. Hum or sing softly to steady your heartbeat and invite calm.

Prayer
Holy Spirit,
Teach me to worship beyond words—in truth, humility, and gratitude.
In Jesus' name, I pray, Amen.

Journal Prompt
How does authentic worship renew your sense of connection with the Holy Spirit?

Affirmation
I worship in my spirit and in truth. The presence of the Holy Spirit fills my spirit with peace.

 DAY 7 – PRAY WITHOUT CEASING

Scripture
Rejoice always, pray continually, give thanks in all circumstances; for this is God's will for you in Christ Jesus.
(1 Thessalonians 5:16–18 NIV)

Reflection
Continuous prayer is not endless talking—it is unbroken awareness of God. The Spirit turns ordinary moments into sacred dialogue: a breath becomes thanksgiving, a sigh becomes surrender.

When you let the Spirit guide your thoughts, prayer becomes as natural as breathing. The conversation never stops; it simply flows beneath the surface of your day. In that communion, dryness fades. You rediscover that prayer is not something you do to reach God—it is what happens when you walk with Him.

Temple Practice
Pause three times today to whisper a simple prayer: "Thank You, Holy Spirit." "Help me, Holy Spirit." "I love You, Holy Spirit."

Health Coaching Tip
Pair breath with prayer. Inhale—"Holy Spirit, You are here." Exhale—"I rest in Your peace."

Prayer
Holy Spirit,
Breathe prayer through me today. Keep my spirit tuned to Your constant presence.
In Jesus' name, I pray, Amen.

Journal Prompt
What everyday activities could become prayer when done with awareness of the Holy Spiritt?

Affirmation
I walk in constant conversation with the Holy Spirit. Prayer is the rhythm of my spirit.

 DAY 8 – SURRENDER YOUR WILL

Scripture
Father, if You are willing, take this cup from Me; yet not My will, but Yours be done.
(Luke 22:42 NIV)

Reflection
Surrender is not loss—it is alignment. Jesus' prayer in Gethsemane reveals holy strength: choosing trust when every emotion resists. The Holy Spirit helps you pray the same way—translating your sighs into surrender.

When life feels uncertain, your spirit clings to control, but peace grows only where will yields to wisdom. To surrender is to rest in the love of God—the Father, the Son, and the Holy Spirit—knowing He chooses what refines, not what destroys. In yielding, you find release; in release, you find realignment.

Temple Practice
Write one area where you are struggling to let go. Pray aloud, "Not my will, Lord, but Yours be done," and release it into His hands through the Holy Spirit.

Health Coaching Tip
Progressive muscle relaxation mirrors spiritual surrender. Tighten and release each muscle group, symbolizing letting go of control.

Prayer
Holy Spirit,
Teach me to trust God's divine plan more than my preferences. Align my will with His will through Your guidance and peace.
In Jesus' name, I pray, Amen.

Journal Prompt
What happens in your emotions when you truly release control to the Holy Spirit?

Affirmation
I surrender my will to His will; the Holy Spirit guides my path.

 DAY 9 – LIVE IN PURPOSE

Scripture
For we are God's handiwork, created in Christ Jesus to do good works, which God prepared in advance for us to do.
(Ephesians 2:10 NIV)

Reflection
The Holy Spirit not only comforts—He commissions. After seasons of suffering, purpose can feel distant, yet God never wastes what He has allowed in your life. Every lesson and every scar becomes a tool in His hands. He works it all together for your good and His glory.

You are God's handiwork, created in Christ Jesus to do good works. You are His masterpiece—molded and shaped for meaning that extends beyond your pain. The Spirit breathes courage where fear once ruled, turning survival into service. When you follow His leading, purpose does not pressure you; it flows naturally from alignment.

Temple Practice
Ask the Spirit, "How can I serve someone today?" Follow the first gentle prompting you sense.

Health Coaching Tip
Serving others releases feel-good endorphins and fosters joy. Small acts of kindness nourish body, soul, and spirit.

Prayer
Holy Spirit,
Reveal the purpose You have prepared for me. Use my restored body, soul, and spirit to bless others and glorify You.
In Jesus' name, I pray, Amen.

Journal Prompt
How has God transformed your pain into purpose?

Affirmation
I walk in divine purpose; my life is God's masterpiece in motion.

 # DAY 10 – REFLECT HIS GLORY

Scripture
And we all, who with unveiled faces contemplate the Lord's glory, are being transformed into His image with ever-increasing glory, which comes from the Lord, who is the Spirit.
(2 Corinthians 3:18 NIV)

Reflection
When Christ died and the veil was torn, God's presence was released from the Holiest of Holies in the Temple of Jerusalem to dwell within you. The Holy Spirit now radiates His glory through your rebuilt temple—body, soul, and spirit. You are transformed from the inside out by the Holy Spirit. You do not have to chase transformation—you simply reflect it.

Every act of love, forgiveness, or faith becomes light shining through healed cracks. The more you contemplate His goodness, the more His image appears in you. This is the ultimate realignment: spirit to Spirit, glory to glory, wholeness to worship.

Temple Practice
Stand before a mirror and whisper, "The Spirit of the Lord lives in me." Smile in gratitude for the glory He reflects through you.

Health Coaching Tip
Smiling releases serotonin and lifts mood—a physical echo of inner joy. Let gratitude show on your face.

Prayer
Holy Spirit,
Thank You for dwelling within me. Let Your light shine through my life so others see Your glory.
In Jesus' name, I pray, Amen.

Journal Prompt
Where do you see glimpses of God's glory shining through your restored spiritual health?

Affirmation
The Spirit of the Lord lives in me; His glory radiates through my rebuilt temple—body, soul, and spirit.

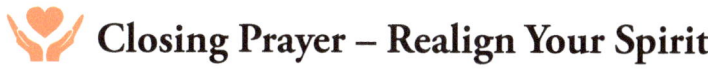 # Closing Prayer – Realign Your Spirit

Holy Spirit,

Thank You for drawing me close and teaching me to dwell in Your presence

You have taken what was weary and crushed, and You have breathed new life into my spirit. You have restored my connection with the Father and renewed my strength through Christ.

Thank You for guiding my steps, whispering truth, and filling me with Your peace. Help me remain sensitive to Your voice and obedient to Your leading. When I am tempted to rely on my own strength, remind me to abide in You. When my passion fades, fan the flame again with Your presence.

May my spirit stay aligned with Yours—rooted in love, grounded in truth, and overflowing with grace toward others. Use my life as a living testimony of Your glory.

Holy Spirit, empower me to walk in Your rhythm and reveal Your glory wherever I go.

In Jesus' name, I pray, Amen.

Continue Your Triune Temple Journey™

Congratulations!

You have completed *Book 3 – Realign Your Spirit: A 10-Day Journey to Spiritual Health and Wholeness* in the *Rebuild Your Temple, God's Way® Faith and Health 10-Day Devotional Series.*

You have begun the transformation process — a journey of healing that continues day by day.

You have rebuilt the *Outer Court* of your Triune Human Temple™ by restoring your body, renewed the *Inner Court* of your temple by healing your soul, and entered the *Holiest of Holies* of your temple by realigning your spirit with God the Father and God the Son through God the Holy Spirit.

During this phase of your Triune Temple Journey™, you discovered that the Holy Spirit is not a distant power but a present companion — your Comforter, Counselor, and Guide.

Your temple is being restored to health and wholeness — not through perfection, but through His continual presence and grace.

Remember: Healing is not a destination; it is a divine rhythm of abiding, trusting, and growing in His grace.

Continue your Triune Temple Journey™ of faith and health by exploring the *Rebuild Your Temple, God's Way® Faith and Health 30-Day Devotional* and the *Rebuild Your Temple, God's Way® Faith and Health Bible Study Workbook*, and by staying connected to God's presence through worship, prayer, and community.

Let **Rebuild Your Temple, God's Way®** continue to guide and support you!

Visit **www.rebuildyourtemplegodsway.com** to explore transformational Christian health coaching programs and resources designed to help you reclaim and maintain a life of health and wholeness—body, soul, and spirit—God's way.

Restore Your Body. Renew Your Soul. Realign Your Spirit.™

www.ingramcontent.com/pod-product-compliance
Lightning Source LLC
Chambersburg PA
CBHW040906120626
46551CB00006B/669